JOURNEY THROUGH
SOUTH
AFRICA

ANITA GANERI

W
FRANKLIN WATTS

Franklin Watts
First published in Great Britain in paperback in 2018 by The Watts Publishing Group

Credits
Editor in Chief: John C. Miles
Series Editor: Amy Stephenson
Series Designer: Emma DeBanks
Picture Researcher: Diana Morris

Picture Credits: Kicrran Allen/Dreamstime: front cover. Patrick Allen/Dreamstime: 16b. Steve Allen/Dreamstime: 5b. American Spirit/Dreamstime: 17tr. Awie Badenhorst/Dreamstime: 23bl. Richard Brooksbank/Dreamstime: 12b. Buzz Pictures/Alamy: 28c. Richard Cavalleri/Shutterstock: 11cr. Checco/Dreamstime: 15c. Cmspic/ Shutterstock: 7tcl. Neal Cooper/Dreamstime: 13t. Delstudio/Dreamstime: 4t. Demerzel21/Dreamstime: 19t. Ulrich Doering/ Alamy: 9c. Domossa/Dreamstime: 29tl. Johan Elzenga/Dreamstime: 3, 10. Four Oaks/Shutterstock: 6bc. Chris Fourie/Shutterstock: 7bl. GFC Collection/Alamy: 20. Hannest/Dreamstime: 13b. L A Hodges/Alamy: 18. icswart/ Shutterstock: 7tr. Gil K/Shutterstock: 17tl. Anan Kaewkhamma/Shutterstock: 6cr. Karelgallas/Dreamstime: 19b. Holger Karius/Dreamstime: 11t. Heiko Kiera/Shutterstock: 22c. Andrey Kuzmin/Dreamstime: 6br. Leksele/ Shutterstock: 6bl. Chris van Lennep/Dreamstime: 23t. Bartosz Lewandowski/Dreamstime: 25t. Francois Loubster/ Dreamstime: 27b. Chris Mattison/Alamy:14b. Milwane Wildlife Sanctuary/Jacques Marais: 21t. Mr Zach/Shutterstock: 7tcl. Ulrich Mueller/Dreamstime: 6cl, 17b. Alexander Mychko/Dreamstime: 23br. Only Fabrizio Shutterstock: 7tcb. Photosky/Dreamstime: 26t. Grobler du Preez/Shutterstock: 6tlb, 12c, 15t. Prisma Bildagentur AG/Alamy: 1, 6t, 9b. Julia Reschke/Shutterstock: 16c. L Sebastian/Dreamstime: 7cb. Nico Smit/Dreamstime: 25b. L M Spencer/ Shutterstock: 28b. stuwdamdorp/Alamy: 7br, 26b. Swinner/Shutterstock: 7ca. Lucarelli Temistocle/Shutterstock: 5c. Times Newspapers/Rex Shutterstock: 9t. Peter Titmuss/Alamy: 14c. Ian Trower/Robert Harding PL: 24. Gerhardus Vermeulen/Dreamstime: 8. whitcomberd/Dreamstime: 27t. Jochen Wijnands/Horizons WWP/TRVL/Alamy: 7tl, 21b. Andrea Willimore/Shutterstock: 4c, 7brb, 29b. Anke van Wyke/Shutterstock: 7bc. Zhukovsky/Dreamstime: 22b. zonefalal/Dreamstime: 7bcb.

Dewey number: 968.068
ISBN: 978 1 4451 3685 1

Printed in Malaysia

Franklin Watts
An imprint of
Hachette Children's Group
Part of The Watts Publishing Group
Carmelite House
50 Victoria Embankment
London EC4Y 0DZ

An Hachette UK Company
www.hachette.co.uk

www.franklinwatts.co.uk

CONTENTS

WELCOME TO SOUTH AFRICA

Siyakwamukela ku South Africa! Welcome to South Africa! Covering an area of 1,221,000 square km, this large country in the southern part of the African continent has beautiful scenery, modern cities and a long and sometimes difficult history. When you think of South Africa, you might imagine exotic animals, world-class cricket and rugby teams, and Nelson Mandela (1918–2013). South Africa is famous for all of these things, and lots more. On your journey you'll take a safari through the Kruger National Park, climb Table Mountain and visit the world's largest diamond mine.

▲ Table Mountain in Cape Town is named for its flat 'tabletop' shape.

Coasts, plains and peaks

Surrounded on two sides by the Atlantic and Indian oceans, South Africa has a long coastline, stretching for more than 2,500 km. It has land borders with six other countries – Botswana, Namibia, Zimbabwe, Mozambique, Lesotho and Swaziland. South Africa has a wide range of landscapes, from high mountains and rolling grasslands, to scorching deserts and vast plains. The climate is temperate – generally warm and sunny – though it is cooler higher up.

Many languages

Siyakwamukela ku South Africa means 'Welcome to South Africa' in Zulu, one of the country's 11 official languages. Among the others are English, Afrikaans and Xhosa. Zulu is spoken by the Zulu people from the province of KwaZulu-Natal (see pages 22–25). Here are some Zulu phrases to try out on your travels:

Sawubona – hello (to one person)

Sanibonani – hello (to several people)

Unjani? – how are you? (to one person)

Ninjani? – *how are you?* (to several people)

Ngiyaphila – thank you

Yebo – yes

Cha – no

▶ Pupils at South African schools learn more than one language to reflect the country's varied culture.

Story of South Africa

By studying the fossils of early humans (see page 17), archaeologists know that people have lived in South Africa for hundreds of thousands of years. But it is South Africa's more recent history that has brought it to the attention of the world. From the 17th century, people from Holland and Britain began to settle in South Africa. Black South Africans were forced off their land and treated very badly. From the 1940s, apartheid – a system that keeps black and white people apart – became law. Black people had few rights, had to go to different schools, use different transport, and live in separate areas.

Apartheid finally ended in 1994, and democratic elections were held in which Nelson Mandela became South Africa's first black president. Today, black and white people are equal in South Africa, but there is still a huge gap between how rich (mainly white) and poor (mainly black) people live.

▼ South Africa's flag was redesigned in 1994 to tie in with the elections. The 'Rainbow Nation' flag represents all of South Africa's people.

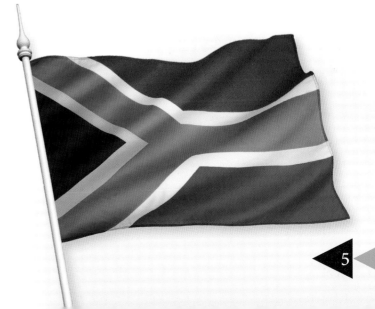

JOURNEY PLANNER

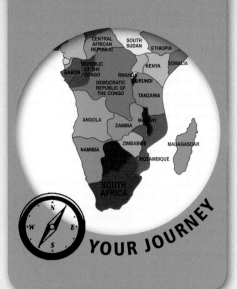

YOUR JOURNEY

1

2

3

(Kgalgadi Transfrontier Par

Kalahari Gemsbok National Park

NAMIBIA

Upington

Orange R

Riemvasmaak Community Conservancy

Springbok

2

Cederberg mountains

Tankwa Karoo National Park

Beaufort We

South Atlantic Ocean

Great Karoo

Langebaan

1

Paarl

Worcester

CAPE TOWN

Stellenbosch

Table Mountain

Somerset West

Cape of Good Hope

Mossel Ba

Cape Agulhas

KEY

—— your route around South Africa

------ flight

—— river

—— road

★ capital cities

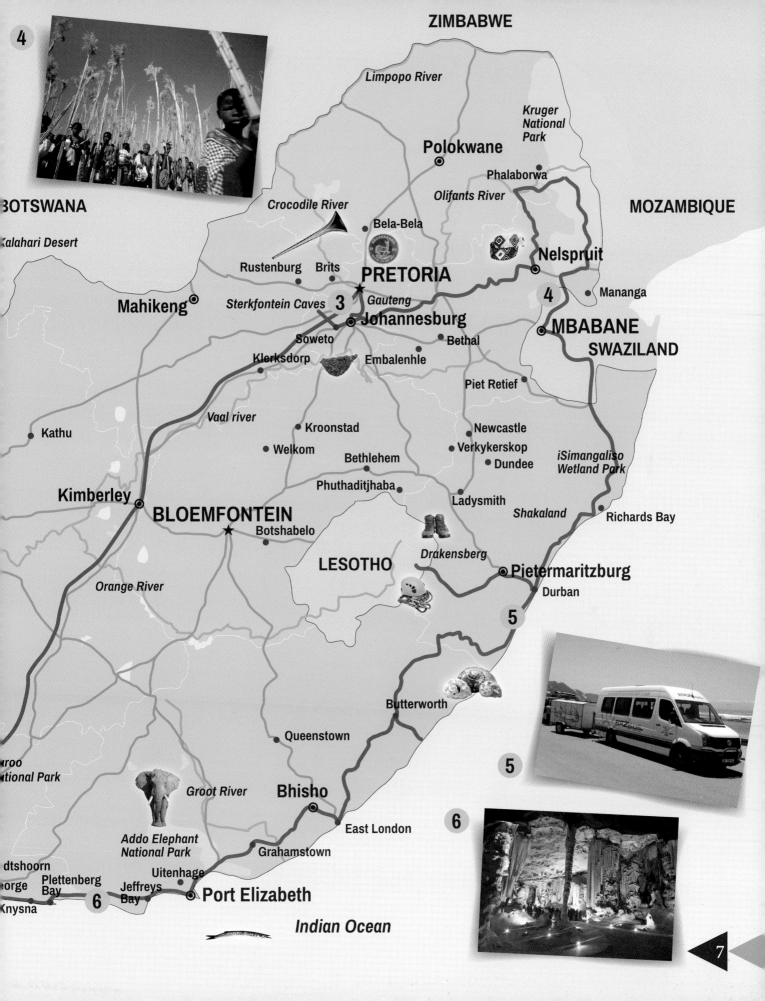

ZIMBABWE

Limpopo River

Kruger National Park

Polokwane ⊙

Phalaborwa

Olifants River

BOTSWANA

MOZAMBIQUE

Kalahari Desert

Crocodile River

Bela-Bela

Nelspruit

Rustenburg   Brits

PRETORIA ★

Mananga

4

Mahikeng ⊙

Sterkfontein Caves **3**

Gauteng

Johannesburg ⊙

MBABANE ⊙

SWAZILAND

Soweto

Bethal

Klerksdorp

Embalenhle

Vaal river

Piet Retief

Kathu

Kroonstad

Newcastle

Welkom

Verkykerskop

iSimangaliso Wetland Park

Bethlehem

Dundee

Phuthaditjhaba

Shakaland

Kimberley

Ladysmith

Richards Bay

BLOEMFONTEIN ★

Botshabelo

Drakensberg

LESOTHO

Pietermaritzburg ⊙

Orange River

Durban

5

Butterworth

Groot River

Queenstown

Karoo National Park

Bhisho ⊙

6

Addo Elephant National Park

East London

Grahamstown

Oudtshoorn

Uitenhage

George

Plettenberg Bay

Jeffreys Bay

Port Elizabeth ⊙

Knysna

6

Indian Ocean

5

6

7

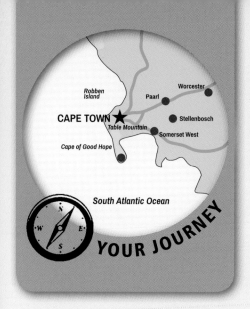

YOUR JOURNEY

ARRIVING IN CAPE TOWN

Your journey begins in the beautiful city of Cape Town on the south-west coast. Your flight will arrive at Cape Town International Airport, which is about 20 km outside the city. Hop on a MyCiTi bus outside the terminal for the short journey into town.

City sights

Cape Town is one of South Africa's biggest cities, with a population of 3.7 million. It is also one of the country's three capitals, alongside Pretoria and Bloemfontein (see page 15). There's plenty to explore and one of the easiest ways to see Cape Town is to catch a City Sightseeing bus. You can hop on and off as you wish. Don't miss the Castle of Good Hope, the oldest colonial building in South Africa. This star-shaped fort was built in the 17th century by Dutch traders to protect them from British attacks.

From the castle, it is a short walk to the Victoria & Albert Waterfront, with its shops, restaurants, aquarium and sweeping views. Built on top of the city's docks, the V&A Waterfront is still a working harbour.

▼ Another view of Table Mountain.

▼ The Castle once stood on the coastline of Table Bay. Today, it is inland because the land in between has been reclaimed from the sea.

Robben Island

From Nelson Mandela Gateway on the Waterfront, catch a ferry to Robben Island, a small, flat island in Table Bay. Be warned – the sea can be choppy, especially in winter. For centuries, the island was used as a prison. Its most famous inmate was Nelson Mandela, an anti-apartheid revolutionary who spent 18 years there after he was convicted of several crimes, including treason. Today, the island is a UNESCO World Heritage Site and the prison is a museum. The first part of the official tour is by bus, and you'll visit places such as the stone quarry, where prisoners were set to work. The second part is a tour of the prison, led by a former prisoner, and ending with a visit to Mandela's prison cell (see below).

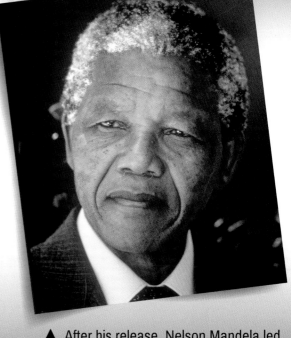

▲ After his release, Nelson Mandela led the ANC to victory in a general election and saw the end of apartheid.

Malay culture

Over the centuries, people from many different countries have settled in Cape Town, including the Dutch and British. They have left a lasting mark on the city. The Cape Malay people are Muslims, whose ancestors came from south-east Asia and who were brought to South Africa by the Dutch as slaves. Their culture, food and ways of worship have left a lasting mark on the city.

▶ Many of the homes in Bo-Kaap – a township in Cape Malay – are painted in bright colours.

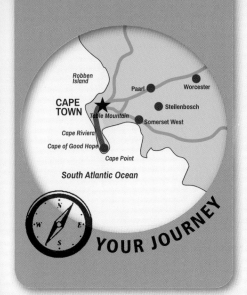

Robben Island
Paarl
Worcester
CAPE TOWN
Table Mountain
Stellenbosch
Somerset West
Cape Riviera
Cape of Good Hope
Cape Point
South Atlantic Ocean

AROUND CAPE TOWN

Cape Town is located on a peninsula that juts out into the South Atlantic Ocean. Its stunning location, spectacular scenery and beautiful beaches make this region South Africa's top tourist destination. To explore the peninsula, hire a car and drive all the way to Cape Point at the tip. The drive is around 160 km long and the roads are good.

▶ Lion's Head

▲ The cable cars turn around as they go up and down, giving panoramic views of Table Mountain, Lion's Head and Cape Town.

Table Mountain

Towering over Cape Town is South Africa's most famous landmark – Table Mountain. At 1,086 m high, it's hard to believe that the flat 'tabletop' (see pages 4 and 8) was once the bottom of a valley! Erosion of the softer rocks of the Cape Fold Mountains over millions of years has left the harder rock exposed. It is often covered in low cloud, nicknamed the 'tablecloth'. You can get to the top by cable car and the trip takes about five minutes. From the cable car station, choose from three hiking trails or join a guided walk.

Scenic drive

The road from Cape Town winds down the Atlantic coast, and takes in Chapman's Peak Drive, a scenic route between Hout Bay and Noordhoek. This stretch is only 9 km long, but the road is cut into the cliff face, with sheer drops to the sea below and towering mountain above. With more than one hundred twists and turns, it's not for the faint-hearted.

▲ Chapman's Peak Mountain has a sandstone top and a Cape Granite bottom. Chapman's Peak Drive sits on top of the hard layer of granite.

Cape Riviera

Heading south out of Cape Town, you drive along a stretch of coast known as the 'Cape Riviera' because of its beautiful sandy beaches. If you fancy sunbathing, swimming or sailing, a stop-off here is a must. Clifton and Llandudno are the most popular beaches, but for surfing, windsurfing and kite-surfing, head a few kilometres further south to Hout Bay, which often has strong winds, and large waves created by the underwater reefs.

Cape of Good Hope

The Cape of Good Hope (see above) is a rocky headland at the south-west tip of the peninsula. People used to think that it was the southernmost tip of Africa, but that is actually Cape Agulhas, further east along the coast. The Cape of Good Hope was named by the Portuguese in the 15th century. They were the first Europeans to sail around it and discover a new trade route to India.

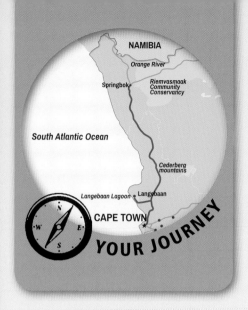

WEST COAST FLOWERS

Your journey continues up the West Coast via an organised 5-day tour. It will take you on a luxury coach from Cape Town, through the dry, sun-baked wilderness of Namaqualand, right up to the Namibian border and then back to Cape Town.

Namaqualand

Despite its hostile appearance, this dry region is full of surprises. From August to October the winter rains fall, and fields of brightly coloured wild flowers burst into bloom, attracting thousands of tourists. You'll also enjoy views of the rugged Cederberg mountains on one side, and the windswept Atlantic coast on the other, as you travel through this stunning region.

▼ During the dry months, flower bulbs lie dormant in the ground. After rain, they quickly sprout and bloom.

▶ An oryx stands among the wild flowers in Namaqualand.

Orange River

The longest river in South Africa, the Orange River flows from the Drakensberg mountains in Lesotho (see pages 24–25) west to the Atlantic Ocean. In the north, it forms part of the border with the neighbouring country of Namibia. The river provides vital water supplies for farming, mining and industry, as well as hydroelectric power.

◀ Great white pelicans use their large bills for scooping up fish.

Bird-spotting tour

A detour along the coastal road takes you to the West Coast National Park. Surrounding the Langebaan Lagoon, this park is one of South Africa's most important wetlands. Don't forget your binoculars – thousands of sea birds roost and breed here on offshore islands. Look out for African penguins, Cape cormorants, Cape gannets, and other aquatic birds, such as lesser flamingos and great white pelicans. You can watch the birds from special hides, dotted around the park.

Seafood snacks

The cold Benguela Current flows north along the West Coast. It brings rich nutrients to the surface, which attract huge shoals of fish, making this an important region for fishing. If you're feeling hungry, head for one of the open-air restaurants (called *skerms*) along the beach. There you can feast on rock lobster, black mussels, angelfish and other delicious seafood.

Cracking rocks

The Cederberg mountains stretch for around 100 km and are famous for their weird and wonderful rock formations. These have been created, over millions of years, by the wind and rain wearing away at the sandstone. Among them are the Maltese Cross, a dramatic 20-m high pillar, and the much-photographed Wolfberg Arch (see below).

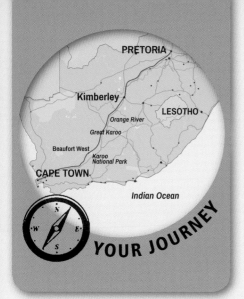

YOUR JOURNEY

CAPE TOWN TO PRETORIA

Back in Cape Town, you board the world-famous Blue Train for the overnight journey to Pretoria in the north-east. It's a long trip of around 1,600 km and takes about 27 hours, but you'll be travelling in style – the train is like a five-star hotel on wheels. You'll have the finest food, and a suite that is a lounge by day and a luxurious bedroom at night.

Great Karoo

The train takes you across the Great Karoo, a vast stretch of dry, dusty land. Very little rain falls on this semi-desert region, although water can be found underground. This has made it possible for people to settle here and set up large sheep and ostrich farms. Enormous herds of antelope, including springbok, also used to roam the Great Karoo but were hunted in huge numbers. Today, they are protected inside a wildlife reserve in the Karoo National Park.

▼ These rocky hills – called Karoo Koppies – are formed from a volcanic rock called dolerite.

▼ A conductress stands in the doorway of a first class carriage on the Blue Train.

The Big Hole measures 1.6 km around its edge and once reached a depth of 800 m.

▼ A view of Pretoria's financial district.

The Big Hole

Before you arrive in Pretoria, the train stops at the town of Kimberley. Diamonds were first found here in 1871, sparking a huge diamond rush. Miners arrived in their thousands to work the 'Big Hole', as the Kimberley Mine became known. Working with only picks and shovels, they dug up millions of pounds worth of diamonds. It was closed as a working mine in 1914 but you can find out about its heyday at the Open Mine Museum. Take a vintage tram tour from the museum to the hole and take a peek into the hole itself from a viewing platform.

University city

Your final stop on the train is Pretoria. You'd be wise to spend a few days here, exploring the city's many historic buildings, theatres, parks and gardens. The city is also a centre of education, with two universities – the University of Pretoria and the University of South Africa, and is home to the South African Reserve Bank.

Three capitals

South Africa is unique as it is the only country in the world with three capital cities. Pretoria is the administrative capital and is home to military and government headquarters, and many embassies. Cape Town is the legislative capital, where laws are made and Parliament actually sits. Bloemfontein is the judicial capital and the Supreme Court is located here. By spreading power over three cities, no single area can become too powerful.

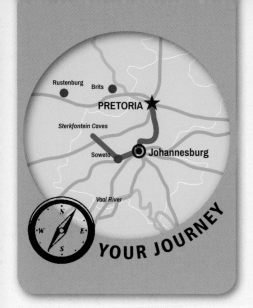

YOUR JOURNEY

PRETORIA TO JOHANNESBURG

The next stop on your journey is the city of Johannesburg, the biggest city (by population) in South Africa. The quickest way to get there from Pretoria is to hop on board one of the new and super-speedy Gautrains. Travelling at up to 160 kph, the train makes the trip in just 35 minutes.

City of gold

Although it is not one of South Africa's capitals, Johannesburg (also known as Jo'burg) is the country's financial and commercial centre and is home to the largest stock exchange in Africa. Its history and importance are closely linked to gold. This precious metal was discovered on a local farm in the late 19th century, and Johannesburg grew quickly from a sprawling tented town into a busy and bustling city. Today, gold (and diamond) exports still play an important part in South Africa's economy. Many mining companies have their headquarters in Johannesburg.

▲ A nugget of gold.

◀ The tall, slender Hillbrow Tower, was decorated with a football in 2010 for the FIFA World Cup.

▲ The Orlando Towers in Soweto are cooling towers from an old coal power station. Today they are covered in murals and you can bungee jump from the bridge between the towers.

Soweto

Soweto is a township on the outskirts of Johannesburg. During apartheid (see page 5), black people were forced to move here, away from the 'whites-only' areas of the city. As more workers arrived, Soweto grew quickly but had problems with overcrowding and poor housing. Many people lived in shacks made from corrugated iron. In the 1970s, Soweto became world famous when students protested against apartheid. The protests turned into riots, and many people were killed or injured. Today, you can take a tour of the township, visiting places such as the Orlando Towers and the house Nelson Mandela lived in before he went to prison (see page 9).

South African sport

A short bus ride from Soweto takes you to Soccer City, the biggest sports stadium in Africa. South Africans are sport mad, and football is particularly popular. With seating for more than 94,000 spectators, the stadium is the home ground of the national football team, and the Kaizer Chiefs – one of South Africa's top teams. In 2010, it hosted the final of the FIFA World Cup.

Cradle of Humankind

About an hour's drive from Johannesburg lie the Sterkfontein Caves (see above). These are home to some of the most famous and important fossils of our ancestors ever found. They include an almost complete skeleton, nicknamed 'Little Foot', which dates back more than 3 million years. A tour guide will take you deep into the cave system.

▲ Soccer City stadium is nicknamed the 'calabash', because it is a similar shape to a calabash gourd.

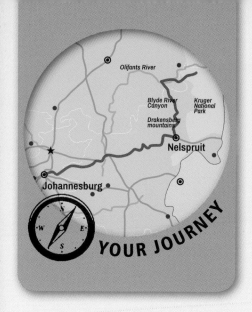

Map labels: Olifants River, Blyde River Canyon, Kruger National Park, Drakensberg mountains, Nelspruit, Johannesburg

WILDLIFE AND CANYONS

Back in Johannesburg, it's time to join your tour bus for the experience of a lifetime – a safari in the Kruger National Park. Your tour guide picks you up in an air-conditioned minibus for the scenic drive to the park. At the entrance gate, you transfer into a safari vehicle, which is open to give you a better view. You'll go on game drives during the day, and stay at a tented camp by night.

The Big Five

The Kruger is one of the largest game reserves in the world, covering around 19,500 square km of savannah grassland in north-eastern South Africa, between the Crocodile and Limpopo rivers. It is famous for the 'Big Five' – elephants, lions, leopards, rhinoceroses and buffalo – as well as giraffes, zebra, hippos and baboons. The best times to see the animals are early in the morning or late in the afternoon, when it is cooler. But each game drive is different and you never know what you might find. Have your binoculars ready!

▼ Typical savannah grasslands have plenty of trees that are widely spaced so there is very little shade.

Formed over millions of years, water has slowly eroded the sandstone, creating the beautiful Blyde River Canyon.

Blyde River Canyon

The town of Nelspruit is a major stopover for visitors travelling to the Kruger National Park. It also marks a handy starting point for a trip to the spectacular Blyde River Canyon in the Drakensberg mountains. This dramatic 25-km-long gash has some of the most dramatic scenery in Africa, with sheer cliffs, lush forests, plunging waterfalls and spectacular rock formations. You can drive or hike around the canyon but, if you're feeling brave, it is also famous for white-water rafting and pot-holing.

Canyon highlights

- Three Rondavels – three huge, round rocks (top right in the picture above), which are thought to look like local huts, known as rondavels.

- God's Window – a popular viewpoint, where the cliffs plunge hundreds of metres to the ground. On a clear day, you can see over the Kruger National Park.

- The Pinnacle – a towering column of rock that rises 3 m above the forest.

- Bourke's Luck Potholes – potholes and plunge pools (see left) carved from the rock by stones and grits carried by the swirling river water.

- Kadishi Tufa waterfall – a 200-m high waterfall. Calcium carbonate deposited from the water has created this rock formation, which looks like a crying face.

19

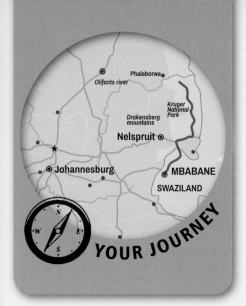

YOUR JOURNEY

KRUGER TO SWAZILAND

From Kruger, take the opportunity to visit the smallest country in southern Africa – Swaziland. You can drive there in a few hours, along good but twisting roads. Swaziland was governed by Britain before becoming an independent country in 1968. Since 1986, its 1.1 million people have been ruled by King Mswati III. Swaziland may be small, but with beautiful scenery, amazing wildlife and rich culture, it is a fascinating place to continue your tour.

Mbabane

Drive to Mbabane, the Swazi capital and largest city. It sits on the Mbabane River, surrounded by craggy hills. The city's economy is based on tourism and sugar exports – sugar is grown here on large plantations. Swaziland is a poor country that relies heavily on trading with South Africa, and most people are farmers or work in industries including forestry and textile manufacturing.

Visit the colourful markets where traditional Swazi arts and crafts, such as paintings, soapstone carvings, batiks and candles are sold. Afterwards, take a hike up nearby Sibebe ('Bald Rock') – a huge granite rock, around 350 m tall. It's a 4-hour round trip to the top. Follow the yellow arrows up and the white dots down, so that you don't get lost.

▶ Sibebe is the second-largest monolith in the world.

▶ Tourists ride alongside zebras in Mlilwane nature reserve.

Swazi nature

Swazi's three nature reserves – Mlilwane, Hlane and Mkhaya – are all worth a visit, and you can reach them easily by bus from the capital. Mlilwane is located in the Ezulwini Valley, the 'Valley of Heaven', an area once used for tin mining. You can explore the park by foot, jeep, mountain bike or on horseback. Further east, Hlane was once a royal hunting ground. Join a guided walking safari to see lions, elephants and rare white rhinoceroses.

Swaziland facts and figures

Area: 17,364 square km
Population: 1,119,000 (2015)
Capital: Mbabane
Ruler: King Mswati III
Official languages: Swazi, English
Currency: South African rand; Swazi lilangeni

Swazi culture

In August or September, thousands of unmarried Swazi girls travel to Ludzidzini, the royal village of the Queen Mother, to take part in an eight-day festival, called Umhlanga ('Reed Dance'). The girls wear traditional costumes, including short skirts and bead necklaces, and carry long reeds. They sing and dance in front of the royal family, and present their reeds to the Queen Mother.

▶ Swazi girls with their reeds at the Umhlanga festival.

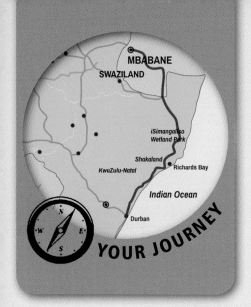

YOUR JOURNEY

SWAZILAND TO DURBAN

Located in a natural harbour on the east coast, the city of Durban is the biggest and busiest port in South Africa. You can reach it by road from Swaziland, driving mostly along the N2 highway. The journey is about 400 km long from Mbabane but there are plenty of places to stop on the way.

Wetland wonderland

A magical place to break your journey is the iSimangaliso Wetland Park, around 275 km north of Durban. The park has an amazing range of habitats, from coral reefs to sand dunes and wetlands, and is home to more than 500 species of birds, 800 hippos and 1,200 Nile crocodiles. If you're there between November and February, join an evening guided walk to watch highly endangered sea turtles come ashore to dig their nests and lay their eggs.

▲ A newly hatched baby leatherback turtle emerges from the sand.

Zulu culture

Durban is the biggest city in the province of KwaZulu-Natal, the home of the Zulu people. To find out more about Zulu life, head down the coast from iSimangaliso to Shakaland, named after the great Zulu king, Shaka. Here, you can visit a Zulu *kraal* (village), a group of round, grass huts, grouped around an enclosure where the cattle, a symbol of wealth in Zulu culture, were kept at night for safety.

► Zulu women outside a traditional hut.

▲ Surfing these huge 'tube' waves takes great skill.

Surf scene

With its warm, sunny weather and Indian Ocean shoreline, Durban is a popular spot for a holiday. Tourists flock to the Golden Mile, a stretch of hotels, restaurants and beaches along the seafront. For something more adventurous, head for Cave Rock Bluff. Here, a reef and an underwater channel produce huge, powerful waves, making this one of South Africa's top surf spots. People come from all over the country to ride the 'tubes' (see above).

▲ The word, potjiekos, translates as 'small pot food'.

South African food

Potjiekos – stew cooked in a three-legged pot (see below, left)

Bunny chow – curry served in a hollowed-out loaf of bread

Bobotie – minced meat baked with an egg-custard topping

Chakalaka – spicy vegetable relish

Umngqusho – a dish made from white maize (corn) and sugar

Biltong – strips of air-dried meat

Bredie – a very spicy stew of meat and vegetables

Melktert – custard tart

▶ Chakalaka

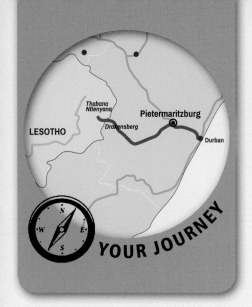

DRAGON MOUNTAINS

For the next few days, Durban acts as your base while you explore the mighty Drakensberg, or 'Dragon Mountains'. The Zulus call the jagged mountains *ukhahlamba*, which means 'a barrier of spears', and it's easy to see why. These are the highest mountains in southern Africa, with names such as Cathedral Peak, Giant's Castle and Mnweni Needles. The highest peak is Thabana Ntlenyana, which is 3,482 m high.

Hiking trails

Thousands of people visit the Drakensberg each year to go hiking, climbing, fishing and birdwatching. Some of the best hiking trails are around Cathedral Peak. Depending on how fit you are, you can choose from an easy route, lasting a few hours and following the Nyosi River, to an extreme hike of three days, along a very steep pass, called Organ Pipes Pass. For something more relaxing, try 'slackpacking' instead. All you have to do is walk the trail while your bags are transported to your campsite.

▼ Hikers on this trail are rewarded with a spectacular view of the flat-topped Cathkin Peak.

Hairpin bends

The Drakensberg run along the eastern border of the country of Lesotho, which you can reach by driving over the Sani Pass. This twisting mountain road zig-zags up through the mountains, in a series of hairpin bends. The Sani Pass began as a donkey track, but today you'll need a 4x4 vehicle and to stay alert at all times. The road is extremely dangerous due to its steep gradient and rough surface, and has claimed many lives.

Lesotho

Once you're safely over the Sani Pass, you enter Lesotho. This mountainous country is completely surrounded by South Africa. It gained its independence from Britain in 1966. Like Swaziland it is a poor country, where most people live by farming, or find work in South Africa. Factories also make clothes for export. Lesotho's main natural resource is water, which is used to produce hydroelectricity for Lesotho and South Africa.

▲ The steep Sani Pass climbs a total of 1,332 m.

San rock art

Around 1,000 years ago, the lush valleys of the Drakensberg were home to the San people. They survived by gathering plants and hunting animals with bows and arrows. Over the centuries, the San were driven out of the area. Today, the only sign of their culture are thousands of beautiful paintings on the walls of caves. The caves are often difficult to reach, but it is worth the trek to see them.

▶ These human figures with animal heads are typical of the San style of rock art.

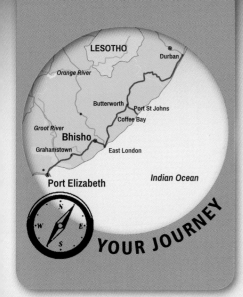

WILD COAST

YOUR JOURNEY

Your journey continues along the south-east coast between Durban and Port Elizabeth. This is a remote part of South Africa and public transport is patchy. Your best option is to catch a Baz Bus. Aimed at travellers on a budget, you buy a ticket and can then hop on and off the bus at various stops along the way. The buses have on-board TVs and DVD players, and there is even space for your bike or surfboard.

▲ The Hole in the Wall at Coffee Bay.

▲ Baz buses have trailers to carry tourists' surfboards and other luggage.

Wild Coast

The stretch of coastline from Durban to East London is known as the Wild Coast. It is famous for its stunning scenery, with beautiful bays, sheer cliffs and rocky headlands. About midway between Durban and East London is the seaside town of Coffee Bay. Legend says that it is named after the coffee trees that grew when a ship carrying coffee beans was wrecked on the shore. It's a great place to go for a hike or a swim, or you can explore the dramatic Hole in the Wall, a huge hole in the cliff carved out by the sea.

Gone fishing

If you're visiting from May to July, head for the town of Port St Johns, north of Coffee Bay. Every year, billions of sardines migrate along the coast, following the ocean currents. The fish form huge shoals (see below) more than 7 km long, which attract predators, such as dolphins, sharks and seabirds. They also attract tourists and fishermen, who catch the sardines in large nets.

Port Elizabeth

In Port Elizabeth, you hop off the bus for the last time. The city is named after the wife of the British governor, Sir Rufane Donkin (1772–1841). Follow the Donkin Heritage Trail around the city to see 50 sights linked to the first British settlers in 1820. They include the City Hall, the Campanile (bell tower), Fort Frederick and the Donkin Reserve, which is a park overlooking the harbour with a stone memorial to Elizabeth Donkin.

The Xhosa

The region around the Wild Coast is the traditional home of the Xhosa people. They speak the Xhosa language, which uses many click sounds. Some of the most famous South Africans of recent times, including Nelson Mandela and Desmond Tutu (1931–), the first black Archbishop of Cape Town, are Xhosa. A Xhosa hymn, *Nkosi Sikelel' iAfrika* (God Bless Africa), is South Africa's national anthem.

▲ Traditional round Xhosa houses are thatched and painted in bright colours.

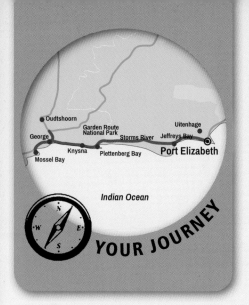

Oudtshoorn

George
Garden Route
National Park
Storms River
Uitenhage
Jeffreys Bay
Knysna
Plettenberg Bay
Port Elizabeth
Mossel Bay

Indian Ocean

YOUR JOURNEY

GARDEN ROUTE

The last leg of your journey takes you along another scenic stretch of coastline from Port Elizabeth to Mossel Bay, following the N2 highway. Between Storms River in the east and Mossel Bay in the west, the road is called the Garden Route. One of the most popular routes with tourists, it passes through picturesque towns, magnificent forests and towering mountains. It takes about 4 days to drive, allowing for plenty of stops.

Forest trails

From Storms River, the road passes through the ancient Tsitsikamma Forest, which grows along the coast. You can follow the 41-km Otter Trail – it takes 5 days, and you spend the nights in comfortable huts. There are some steep climbs so you need to be fit. If you're still feeling energetic at the end, head for Bloukrans Bridge. It stands 216 m above the river, and is the site of the world's highest bungee jump.

► Clouds can form under the 216-m high Bloukrans Bridge.

▲ Adventurous visitors to Tsitsikamma Forest can take a zip line route through the canopy.

▶ People live on islands, such as Leisure Island (top) and Thesens Island (bottom), in the middle of Knysna Lagoon.

Oyster Festival

Further along the route, you reach the town of Knysna, which stands on the shore of a river estuary, known as the Knysna Lagoon. This opens into the ocean through two huge cliffs, nicknamed 'the Heads'. The lagoon is famous for its oysters and, every June, visitors flock to the town for the Oyster Festival. The festival lasts for 10 days and around 200,000 oysters are eaten.

Ostrich ride

Further along the coast, turn off the main road and head into the mountains along the Swartberg Pass. This spectacular 24-km gravel road was built by prisoners in the 1880s. Follow the pass to Oudtshoorn, famous for its ostrich farms. The town grew rich in the 1870s from the sale of ostrich feathers for hats and fans. Today, ostriches are still farmed here for their eggs, meat and leather. You can visit an ostrich farm and even ride in an ostrich derby.

Cango Caves

Round off your South African journey with one final stunning geological formation. Close to Oudtshoorn are the Cango Caves, with their extraordinary stalactites and stalagmites. The narrow tunnels and huge chambers reach for more than 4 km underground, although visitors are only allowed into the first part. Here you can marvel at Cleopatra's Needle (see above), which stands 9 m tall and is thought to be 150,000 years old.

GLOSSARY

administrative
Describing how a business, government or country is managed or run.

ANC
African National Congress. The political party that now rules South Africa.

apartheid
Official government policy in South Africa that separated black and white people, and treated them differently.

archaeologist
A person who studies the past from human and animal remains, and other ancient objects.

bungee jump
Activity in which someone jumps from a high bridge on the end of a rubber rope.

calcium carbonate
A white crystal found in some rocks.

colonial
Describing a time when other countries ruled South Africa.

current
A huge river of water flowing through the ocean; it can be hot or cold.

democratic
System of government in which a country is governed by ministers who are elected by the people of the country.

dormant
Sleeping or not active.

endangered
When an animal or plant is in danger of becoming extinct (dying out forever).

erosion
When rocks and soil are worn away by the action of water, wind, ice and so on.

estuary
Wide channel of a river where it flows into the sea.

gourd
A large dried fruit that is scooped out and used for cooking in or drinking from.

gradient
The degree of steepness of a slope or road.

granite
A very hard volcanic rock that is mainly made up of the minerals quartz, feldspar and mica.

hairpin bends
U-shaped bends in a road that curve back in the opposite direction very sharply.

hydroelectric
Electricity that is produced by the power of running water.

judicial
Describing how justice is carried out in a country.

lagoon
A stretch of water separated from the sea by a coral reef or a low sandbank.

legislative
Describing how laws are made in a country.

monolith
A very large single block of stone.

oryx
A large antelope with long horns that lives in dry regions of Africa and Asia.

panoramic
A wide view of something, such as a landscape.

peninsula
A narrow piece of land that juts out into the sea.

plantation
An enormous farm where crops, such as bananas, are grown.

president
The head of state of a country called a republic.

reclaimed
Land along the coast that has been drained so that it can be farmed and built on.

revolutionary
Person who works to overthrow a government policy or system.

sandstone
Sedimentary rock made of sand or quartz grains that have been compressed together.

stalactite
Long column of calcium carbonate that hangs down from a cave ceiling.

stalagmite
Long column of calcium carbonate that grows up from a cave floor.

township
Planned settlement outside a city for black people to live in.

treason
The crime of betraying your country, especially by trying to overthrow the government.

vintage
Old-fashioned or dated.

BOOKS TO READ

Lonely Planet South Africa, Lesotho and Swaziland (Travel Guide) by James Bainbridge (Lonely Planet, 2015)

Eyewitness Travel Guide: South Africa (Dorling Kindersley, 2015)

The Rough Guide to South Africa, Lesotho and Swaziland (Rough Guides, 2015)

Eyewitness Top 10 Travel Guide: Cape Town and the Winelands by Philip Briggs (Dorling Kindersley, 2014)

Lonely Planet Cape Town and the Garden Route by Simon Richmond (Lonely Planet, 2015)

Been There: South Africa by Annabel Savery (Franklin Watts, 2014)

Countries Around the World: South Africa by Claire Throp (Raintree, 2012)

The Real: South Africa by Moses Jones (Franklin Watts, 2016)

Unpacked: South Africa by Clive Gifford (Wayland, 2015)

WEBSITES

http://www.roughguides.com/destinations/africa/south-africa/

This Rough Guide website is packed with interesting and useful information for your visit. There are tips on where and when to travel, things to see and not to miss, and ideas for lots of great itineraries to inspire your own journey around South Africa.

http://www.lonelyplanet.com/south-africa

Lonely Planet's website is a great introduction to South Africa, and tells you about the best places to visit, historical and geographical information, food and drink to sample, and practical hints and tips about money, health, language and local customs.

https://travelguide.michelin.com/africa-and-indian-ocean/south-africa

This website from Michelin provides all the information you'll need for a fascinating and safe journey around South Africa. Follow some alternative travel routes, take your pick from loads of travel activities and check out the best places to stay.

https://www.gov.uk/foreign-travel-advice/south-africa

It's always a good idea to check out the official government advice before you make any journey abroad. You can find out the latest news and information about South Africa on this UK government website.

Note to parents and teachers:
Every effort has been made by the Publishers to ensure that the websites in this book are suitable for children, that they are of the highest educational value, and that they contain no inappropriate or offensive material. However, because of the nature of the Internet, it is impossible to guarantee that the contents of these sites will not be altered. We strongly advise that Internet access is supervised by a responsible adult.

INDEX